Welcome To my Journey, I hope you enjoy my life Experiences.

Sheila Sampare Gosnell

THE DREAMER
A Book of Collected Poems

SHEILA E. SAMPARE

Order this book online at www.trafford.com
or email orders@trafford.com

Most Trafford titles are also available at major online book retailers.

© Copyright 2014 Sheila E. Sampare.

All rights reserved. No part of this publication may be reproduced, stored in a retrieval system, or transmitted, in any form or by any means, electronic, mechanical, photocopying, recording, or otherwise, without the written prior permission of the author.

Printed in the United States of America.

ISBN: 978-1-4907-4486-5 (sc)
ISBN: 978-1-4907-4487-2 (e)

Because of the dynamic nature of the Internet, any web addresses or links contained in this book may have changed since publication and may no longer be valid. The views expressed in this work are solely those of the author and do not necessarily reflect the views of the publisher, and the publisher hereby disclaims any responsibility for them.

Any people depicted in stock imagery provided by Thinkstock are models, and such images are being used for illustrative purposes only.
Certain stock imagery © Thinkstock.

Trafford rev. 08/19/2014

 www.trafford.com

North America & international
toll-free: 1 888 232 4444 (USA & Canada)
fax: 812 355 4082

This Book is Dedicated to My
Mother Jane Everalda Sampare (Deceased) My Brother
Ronnie Dean Sampare (Deceased)

Contents

The Dreamer 1
Silent Tears 2
Hunger 3
My Love 4
The Nass Valley 5
Need or Greed 6
Nature 7
Northern Lights 8
My Feathered Friend 9
Education 10
The Leader 11
Nisga'a Aim 13
The Homeless 14
My Daughter 15
The Wall 16
A Picture 17
Racism 18
Whispering Winds 19
Night Flight 20
Dad 22
1992 Olympics 23
Lost Souls 24
Sisters 25
Our Father 26
Christina 27
Darlin' 28
Desert Storm 29
A Cry for Peace 30
Victory Dance 32
The Lonely Man 33

Friends	34
A Breath of Life	35
Run Away	36
Mother	37
My Best Friend	38
Sweetie	39
A Daughters Wish	40
Ron	41
Cry Not I Ask	42
A Thankful Thought	43
Deception	44
Waterfalls	45
Space	46
Summers Walk	47
Common Grounds	48
Silent River	49
Unity	51
Distant Friends	52
A Vision	53
Bro'	54
My Baby	55
I Remember	56
Obsession	58
Truth	59
Pain and Happiness	60
Two Ships	61
Pressures	62
Be Cool	63
Dreams	64
The Worker	65
Our Love	66
Godmother	67
Faith	68
It is I	69
Nkwana	70
Beauty of the Night	71

Love Me	72
Joy of My Life	73
A Christmas Wish	74
A Love Found But Lost	75
Don't Take That	76
I say	77
I'd Be Lying	79
If I Could	80
Love is Mystical	81
Lunar Eclipse 2010	82
My Life	83
My Love for You Both	84
One Wrong Decision	85
Some Kind of Love	86
Tonight	87

The Dreamer

As the moonlight shines over the mountain
peaks, so shines the dreamers dream,
Reflecting over his life's needs
Dreaming of all the things that one can have, only
wishing that one day his dreams may come true
As he looks back into his past seeing how his life
has been oh so difficult, he gazes out into
The moonlit skies to dream that dream of
expectancy, of wanting what he can not have
But, only in his dreams.
As the stars light up the heavens and thee clouds
float peacefully amongst the stars
All sharing the beauty of the night.
If only he could see into his future and foresee
all the joy that is coming his way,
Then he would not have to dream his way
through each moonlit night.
As the moon sets down behind the highest
mountain peak setting its final glow
Down onto the earth, so do his dreams fade
away into the early morning's dawn.
Then he awakes to find it was yet another one of his dreams,
dreams of hoping for what he wants out of life. As he opens
his eyes and gazes out the window, he hears a voice;
A voice of hope telling him that he can have
all that he desires out of life,
He just has to go out and get it, and not dream
his way through each moonlit night,
The Dreamer

Silent Tears

A silent love is a cry for help, if there is no communication
Someone's walking, always keep those lines open
Never let your love be silent, if you hear someone crying lend an ear
To hear why there's tears to a silent love

Hunger

The silent cries of hunger grows louder as the pain gets stronger
Our stomachs are empty, so are our pockets.
What can we do? No one will give a helping hand
We are striving so hard to get by
My babies are crying mommy my tummy hurts, but I have
Nothing to offer but a cup of water.
Can we live off our faith? Is it strong enough to get us through a day?
When the night silently passes us by, we are
Awakened by the roars of our stomachs, why must this
Hunger linger with us? Must it be our shadow, never leaving our
Sides, just haunting us down to the ground.

My Love

There never has to be a day that you feel I do not love you any more,
You never have to question my love for you
Or wonder if there is another.
Darlin there's only you, from the beginning to this day
My love has only been in your heart where we'll never be apart
I know there are days when I do not express
my love openly, but it is always
In my heart whereas you are the only one who has the key
To open it.
If you should ever feel the need for my love
when I'm not around, just bring
Your hand to your chest and feel my heart beat with yours,
And hear my voice say that I love you and I'm here for you.
Don't ever question my love for you, I love
you more than words can express
So don't ever feel depressed, for there is nothing or no one that will
Take your place, My Love you are mine and I am yours
Til death do us part

The Nass Valley

As I sit here high above the world, gazing down into our beautiful
Nass Valley I see the tree's as tall as can be their colors
As rich in green as they sway in the cool summers breeze.
While down below them quietly runs the shimmering streams
Passing through our lovely green meadows as they
Nurture every living plant.
Alongside these shimmering streams are wild flowers blooming
Under the sun's rays, showing all the true colors that
Nature can ever produce.
Spread out alongside the mountains are the historic lava beds
Running for miles across the valley.
After all these years of aging are now showing the true beauty
Of our valley, bringing back to life the beauty it once lost,
Now it has regained its strength to reproduce
What has been lost for years.

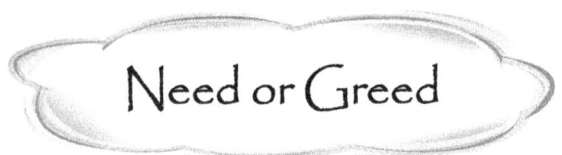

Need or Greed

One man's need is another man's greed, If I were to plant a seed
To every man's need, that would be a great task indeed.
In this destructive world one only has to
defend his seeds, as the world
Slowly crumbles around us.
We listen to our leaders say, Give peace
a chance and keep hope alive,
Through their determination and the will to survive
Would be a great blessing indeed.
We must stand strong and plant those seeds for a brighter tomorrow
Let those seeds bring forth a whole new generation that we will
Teach there is no need for greed in this society.
Let us cast out this desire for greed and precede our needs together
For generosity will preserve our planet
Expelling the need for greed is the most powerful deed any
Man can achieve.

Nature

The river is swollen to its fullest, running
wild and free over our land
Destroying all of nature's beauty in its path.
While the four winds demolish everything as it sweeps
over our homes, plucking everything from the ground.
Quietly but out of control the fires destroys everything it touches,
The tall green trees are lit up like candles,
this action due to recklessness
Of one individual.
While in some parts of the world the sun
is a scorcher, causing no water to
Produce food and plants, for the sun is like an oven with
No temperature control.
We can only wonder is this what the creator
intended mother nature to be?
One that destroys all the beauty of her creation.
The destruction of the waters as they flood
our homes, the fires that burn away
The forests, the sun that disintegrates the lands
And the winds that carry away everything
one worked so hard to build.
Is this what we call nature?

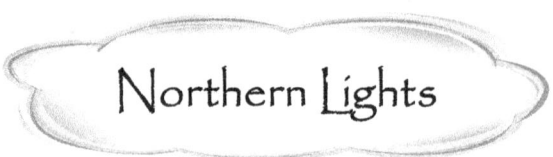

Northern Lights

Northern lights they shine so bright on a moonlit
night, oh what a sight they bring us.
Flashing across the Canadian skies which brings
a tear of amazement to my eyes.
Our nights are cool and crisp as they sway across into the night,
Portraying all the beauty of breathless rays of colored lights, what a
Terrific sight they enlighten us with.
The stars sit peacefully amongst these
layers of light bringing a perfect
Picture down to earth.
Northern lights what a delight to have them
on a wonderful show for everyone
To gaze upon
As each winter month comes and goes.

My Feathered Friend

As a new day approaches with the warmth of the sun shining
Down upon the melting snow.
I see you sitting outside my window singing
your cheerful songs, sung softly
As the warm winds carry it through my open window.
You sit there gracefully high in the trees as the spring breeze
Quietly melts away the winters freezing days.
You sing your songs letting us know that
our winter days are gone and
Spring is here for all to enjoy.
As you sit there singing your songs you bring the feeling of spring
Into my home, my feathered friend.
As the sun descends behind the mountain tops,
the shadows are growing longer,
As you spread your beautiful wings and fly away to your small
And graceful home, until tomorrow comes,
Then I shall open my window and watch
you fly to your favorite tree,
To sing for me once again, so farewell my feathered friend,
Until the sun rises high in the afternoon skies.

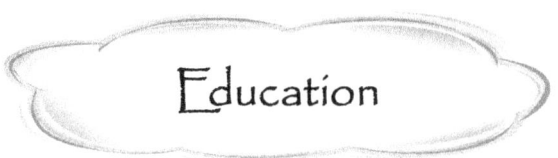

Education

Education is the most important step one must
take in today's changing environment,
With the technology and expertise of the human discovery
One must be well educated.
The knowledge in the books are such an
important tool of every student
And teacher, who have to learn the facts of a good education
To get a good career.
Though there are few people out there who think education is a
Waste of their time, it is through their lack of interest
Will their future will be darkened with
no job to help them survive in
This society of technology
If the opportunity is there to get the education you need,
Grasp it as it makes itself available, for it is
the door to a brighter tomorrow.
It will only take a few years to complete, but the rewards of the few
Years will bring you wealth and happiness.
As education is the way of life take it serious now, your
Future depends on it.

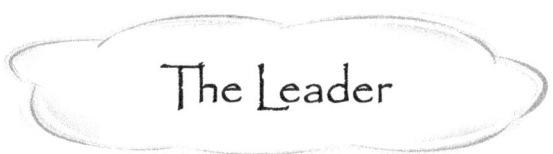

The Leader

Standing distinguished in the silver glow of a
moonlit night, as he stretches his head
High into the skies, letting his followers
know who is the dominant one.
His howl is loud and demanding as the four winds
Carry it through the darkened forests, making sure that all the other
Predators in the wild hear him.
For he is the leader who rules the wild, as he
guides his followers to the land of
Plenty, he is as wise as the owl and strong as the bear.
His strength has brought him out of dangerous grounds for years,
He is a proud and humble leader that everyone near fears.
As he sits there howling into the moonlit
night he prepares his wolf pack for a
Journey they must take, in order to survive and stay clear of those
Who may threaten, the hunters who hunt
for the fur or trophies on their
Walls, a leader must take care of his own to survive in the wild
The Wolf a leader

Frog & Raven Carving
by Frank C. Gosnell

Nisga'a Aim

To win the land claims is the Nisga'a Aim,
this is no game we are playing
It all depends on what our leaders are saying.
For years the Nisga'a have been fighting
this battle, which one day will
Bring tears of victory to our land.
The Nisga'a's shall be forever strong for they
are never wrong, our history has
Been passed down from generation to generation.
Our confidence shall one day prove who
is the dominant one, when this
Day comes we shall remember as a fighting nation that,
Through the years we never backed down
Or lost that spirit of the great warriors.
It has always been our ancestors aim to win, to win this battle they
Started years ago, and so shall we prove to
the world that unity can and will
Over rule all those who doubted us.
As our ancestors said from time immemorial, is we stand together
And be strong we will achieve whatever task we have to
This task is to win the land claims.

The Homeless

They walk the streets day and night looking
for a dark and lonely place
To lay their heads down to rest.
Wandering aimlessly in our cities midst,
while the fortunate ones try
So hard to ignore them as they only ask for a dollar
For a cup of coffee.
They are very eager to grasp that last piece of pride they have left, as
People turn away, because of their ragged
clothes and the smell of the streets
From where they slept last night.
Why; oh why? Can't we stop for a moment to help those who are
Less fortunate, the homeless.
If the world has so much money to spend on things
less important than a human life, why can't
We put a little to help those who need it?
Let us stop wasting our money and spare a dollar or two to help
Rebuild their future, for they are just as human as you and I.

My Daughter

You are my inspiration to life, you bring
sunshine into my rainy days,
As each day passes us by you are blooming so beautiful,
As thee roses bloom on a hot summers day.
When I look at you growing so tall and
beautiful, I can see your smiling face
Which can overcome any of your friend's moody days.
My daughter you are so precious to me, I
cherish every moment that we
Share as you are growing up.
As I look into your playful but mature
eyes, I see a part of me growing
With you
My daughter you are my inspiration to life.
May your beauty and knowledge always bring good fortune to you in
Life, let the sun always shine for you,
For you are someone very special to me.

The Wall

Each stone removed represents each soul
set free, falling to the ground
Like bombs destroying their homes.
Who could have imagined that it would take a wall to
Divide and break the unity of mankind.
Hearts were broken as their homes were invaded
As the innocent souls were stripped of equality,
When they tried so hard to live a normal life.
How can anyone be so cruel as to try and rule someone else's life?
And to live a normal life without any
Regrets?
As time goes by all wounds are healed and the leadership replaced,
The eyes of the wise were opened, they realized
That this wall must come down, and so it did.
From the wise freedom and unity were reborn, every stone removed
Was a relief, so was a new beginning of a new country,
Which was darkened by the Wall.

A Picture

A painting tells a thousand stories as the artist creates a perfect
Picture of reality, every stroke of his brush
expresses a meaning, every color
Is an experience of the artist life;
Who creates a master piece of an emotional state of mind.
Each portrait is sending out all the positive vibes as we see it in the
Beautiful master piece as it is captured within his sentimental values
Of experience.
An artist is like a poet, they both capture the point of expressions to
Send out to those who read and see the little things in life.
As one creates a master piece through his brush
and the other expresses his thoughts
Through a pen,
Both portraying the beauty of life.

Racism

The generation of today is in so much denial
there are people out there,
Who cannot accept our changing environment
We are all equals in this human society, why must this be so hard
To accept? What one must see is we
Do things differently.
To watch this happening around the world, is so sad, as people
Are put down because of the color of their color
Or nationality.
Why must there be judgement against those who are less fortunate?
Why must their privileges be taken away?
We must open our eyes for the future generations that
Will bring fort our nations.
We must let this plague lie down to rest and equality precede
Into a brighter tomorrow.

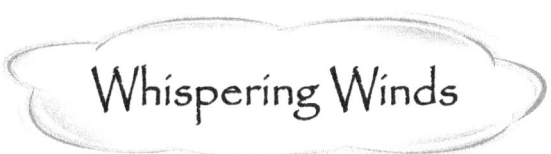

Whispering Winds

Whispering winds speak softly to me, bring good news from the
World around.
Whisper in my ears the secrets around me, let the truth be known
Through the gentleness of your touch
Let the warmth of your breeze caress me as you speak softly
Like a true friend you are to me, Ty whispering winds.
Coming from four corners of the world, travelling here and there
With no doubt about what you heard or seen.
Carrying with you the news good or bad I will never be sad for you
Speak the truth.
You never fail to stop and talk to me as you passing through
Whispering winds.

Night Flight

Letting your wings carry me high above
the clouds as I put all my trust
Into your metal wings, having but one fear
in my heart as never to be up here
I try so hard to keep my cool as we fly through the open skies.
My heart beats faster the higher we soar
into the moonlight, wondering
What if I never make it to my destination or should
I be here?
Flying high above the world that is drifting away from me as I fly in
My night flight.
I sit here looking out my window watching the day slip into night,
Sun reddish orange the
Clouds resting peacefully in the blue skies.
I can only imagine and create the beauty of the night flight
Like an artist creates a master piece so do I capture,
With my pen, bringing to life the beauty of a hot summers night.

Ravens Pride Artwork
by Albert M. Stephens

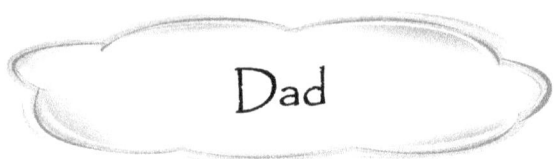

Dad

He has always being a super dad working
every day of his life, on a noisy
Machine that should have drove him crazy, but no not dad for he
Has always being a workaholic.
He'd work so hard and hide the pain of
exhaustion just so his children
Would have food on the table and clothes on their back
Though they were seven of us crazy kids you'd never hear a
Complaint for he loved each one of us equally never did he treat
One better than the other.
As the years passed him by all his children
grew up and have children of their
Own, one would think that dad would get some rest
But no he keeps on working, now for his grandchildren
Whom he treats as his own.
My dad the logger for so many years has only the fear of not having
The money to support his family
I thank God for my dad whose heart is as big as the world.

1992 Olympics

Athletes from the world around have been
training every day preparing
Their bodies and mental conscience for that once
In a life time experience, the Olympics.
Pushing their bodies to the point of perfection to have a shot of
Been the best in the world.
All travelling far and near to get to the city, Barcelona where
Dreams will come true and heroes be made known.
Win or Lose it is the fact that they made it this far as they proved not
Only to themselves, but to the world it
Could be done
For those who came out on top we shall acknowledge their power
Strength and determination
For those who weren't so fortunate to receive medals, their rewards
Will be the memories of the games, the new friendships created
And their ability to participate is a reward
Itself.
1992 Olympics the perfect example that the world can be united

Lost Souls

As I drift aimlessly in the open heavens
wandering around with no place
To call home
My crying soul is floating through heavens open doors wishing for
A descent place to rest my weary soul.
Why, oh why was I so ignorant all the times I was warned
Not to lose control of my life.
Why didn't I stop to think that all the wrong I was doing would
One day take my life away, leaving me with
A wandering soul lost for eternity because of
Negligence.
Joining thousands of lost souls out there
all searching for that peaceful
Place to lie down to rest

Sisters

Throughout the years friends have come and gone like the wind,
Leaving behind only the memories of a
Brief friendship.
While you are out there trying to find a friend that will be
With you through the good times
As well as the bad times, only to encounter
That last the length of your breath.
You sometimes forget that the true friends
you can ever have are your
Sisters, they are always there to bring you up
When you are feeling down, and always have the right advice
You are looking for
Your sisters are the next best thing to a mother, unlike the friends
You may have had in the past, they will be
Truthful especially when you really need to hear the truth
But cannot take it from anyone else.
Whenever you need a friend to lean on
just remember that your sisters
Are just around the corner
Talk and they will listen, cry and they will never turn their
Backs on you for your sisters are your best friend till the end.

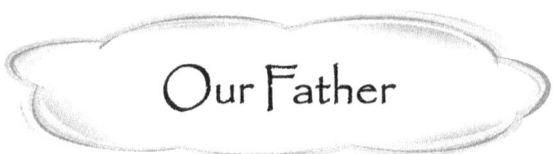

Our Father

Our father who art in heaven make this a better
place to live take into consideration
Our children who must bring forth this world into tomorrow,
Let there be no more sorrow should there be one man seeking to
Borrow, let there be someone to give a helping hand.
Our father who art in heaven let there be peace amongst our midst
So this world will not explode into a blitz
Let them who are at war realize that the whole world is at stake
And not to make that dreadful mistake to nuke us all
Our father who art in heaven give us our
daily guidance that will carry
Us through a day without making any mistakes
Our father who art in heaven give me the strength to carry on with
My purpose in life, that through my writing everyone
Shall realize that this world is in a dreadful state
Amen

Christina

She was small and delicate so fragile to hold, like a rose blooming
So beautiful and carefree, that is how she was to me
Precious as a gem stone, he little smile would light up anyone's day
For she had very little to say, but just
Her expressions told you all you needed to know as her
Youth and innocence was a blessing for she was only a baby
Living in a world for a short time
Her cry was never loud or unpleasant only a whisper in the wind
Family and friends loved and cared for her deeply
She was everyone's little angel
Christina
The gentleness of her touch has captured everyone's loving arms as
The silence of her tiny feet walking towards you
With a smile that came from heaven, no one could not resist but to
Pick her up
She is a gem so precious that we will cherish each memory in our
Hearts and minds forever

Darlin'

We've come a long way and to this day we
are still in so much love, the road
Was never paved of gold which I was told from the
Beginning.
We definitely had our rainy days but our
love was a concrete foundation
That withheld all those shaky grounds
Let our love forever be strong and our relationship last a life time
For it is no crime to be in love the way we are.
Darlin' our love is but a rose the beauty will always be protected
By its thrones where no one will ever reach us
Or bring us down, for we will always be crowned with the
Riches love around
Babe I can tell you this that my love is only in your heart and we will
Never be apart, you can never wonder if
There is another for my love is true to only you till death do us part
So Darlin' always keep in your heart and mind that
I am the only one for you.

Desert Storm

The roaring thunder of the tankers invade the empty streets of Iraq
As the air is filled with constant fear of what or
Who will get bombed next?
The nights are darkened and still, only until the bombs and guns
Start buzzing in the air blasting all through the desert.
As men and women sit patiently waiting and watching to see
Where the next one will fall all praying they would make it home
Safely to their loved ones.
Tis' through their heroic ambition to stay and help those
In danger
Their bravery has earned them great respect and honor,
That will be written down in the history books
The heroes of Desert storm, is a war that shouldn't have happened
But did.

A Cry for Peace

Let there be peace amongst us, peace that
will bring ease to our minds
And freedom for eternity, let us stop this destruction
Peace that will produce unity for the world
around, the one thing this
Planet needs to nurture so we may grow with
Security and be free from all man kinds mistakes.
Peace that will bring forth the spring flowers,
Blossoming every so beautiful, peace that will be carried with the
Four winds throughout this land
Peace that is pure as the winter's snow falling quietly to the ground
Let our cry for peace be heard and
Open the eyes of the fighting leaders that they may see the
Beauty it possess.
Let there be peace so powerful that when we walk down the streets
We will not be afraid, let our cry be so loud
That it can be heard from one end of the world to the other
Let\s just give peace a chance.

Howling Wolf Artwork
by Albert M. Stephens

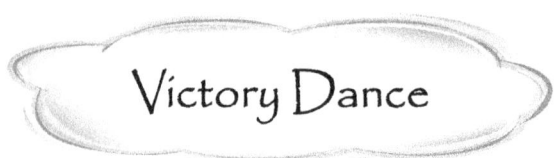

Victory Dance

The gleam of victory was in their eyes as
they gazed into the night skies
Happiness was dancing in their voice as they rejoiced together
From the gleam in their eyes and
The happiness in their voice brought out the victory dance
Of the northern lights dancing so gracefully above us,
Dancing amongst the stars that lit up the night
Everything fell into place the night was
perfect to have a victory dance
At a glance I seen a falling star not far from
Where I was standing.
When the music ended and our friends departed so did the
Northern lights fade away across the moonlit sky

Dedicated to G.A.C.

The Lonely Man

He sits there high on the mountain top watching over our beautiful
Valley for he is the true caretaker of this land.
As vehicles come and go he is there to
guide them over the lava beds,
Through the years has age a great deal, just as the lonely man,
He sits there high in the sky with no one to talk to
For he is the lonely man.
With only the company of the pure white snow as his
Security blanket, which comforts him all winter long.
As the summer's sun gets hotter his image slowly fades until there
Is no more snow left on the mountain top?
Then he is gone for the summer months
Until the fresh winters snow falls once again then his
Face will appear to watch over our valley once more, the lonely man
The care taker of the Nass Valley

Friends

Just the four of us sitting here sharing and confiding in what only
True friends can do.
As we sit here listening to music and what each other has to say
We shut off the outside world in order
To enjoy that unique friendship we created
Each giving and sharing our deepest understanding.
Exchanging our true feelings with no one taking control
Of one's ability to speak,
For our security of our friendship is honesty and the truth.
That is what friends are for to be there when you need them
True friends are the best friend
You cannot find them anywhere else but by your
Side
May our friendship be with us for a life time let us preserve it
And nurture it with all the love and happiness around.
Even when we disagree with one another which is rarely there,
We must keep in our hearts that we are friends
Who are always there no matter what?
Comes in our path.

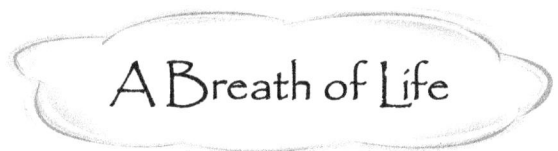

A Breath of Life

You are the breathe of my life you nurture me with your warm
And loving emotions,
I can see the outside world through you, with the tenderness
Of your voice, I can tell you are
Someone very special to me as I am to you.
Mommy, I can only hope you love me as much as I love you
For you can feel me growing inside of you
Every day.
Mother please, oh please give me a chance to live, I will show
You just how much my love means to you,
I promise your world will be much more filled with me around
When you can see just how lovable I am
Mommy please stop and think about what you are going to do,
Not only will you take my breath away you too shall
Feel the pain and bare that guilt always.
So please let me live and grow with every breath you take
You won't make that mistake give me a chance to
Prove my love mommy dear.

Run Away

The streets are filled with runaway's,
running away from their family
Problems, each looking for a place to hide from all
Of life's mishaps.
Through lack of communication in our society that these children
Are forced to turn to the streets.
They need the understanding and love from those close to them,
To help get them through this fast
And changing pace of life.
Sometimes things happen unpredictable
for them, they need a chance to
Be young and free of all pressures.
With the problems of drugs and alcohol in today's society they
Feel that need to challenge of being straight or
To be addicted,
Not only are those the two main factors, there is also their
Education trying so hard to achieve that goal,
To maintain a better life.
So they are faced with all of life's pure pressures that they
Find so difficult to cope with,
And the only way out for them is turning to
The streets.

Mother

There is no other who could fill your shoes, I'll never choose anyone
But you for you are my mother,
Through all the years of growing up I can remember how much you
Loved us all, you taught us well and that was
To respect those around us.
Oh how I loved your home cooked meals
that were plenty of, from babes
Mother you were always there to comfort and protect us.
And the way you cooked and cleaned showed us just how much
You really cared for us.
The tenderness in your voice reflected the gentleness that was
Taught to each one of us as each day passed
Your eyes and ears were open to
Our needs.
Mother your love was always plentiful, enough to share with all
Seven of your crazy children, who at times
Gave you the biggest headaches but you never complaint.
What you taught us we now teach our
children and grandchildren, whom
You know love you just as much as we do.

My Best Friend

We've being friends since grade school we
spent every minute together
Laughing and helping one another out,
We shared everything that we had material and the truest of true
Our friendship.
What a life we had growing up things came to us so easily
We never had the time to look for the things we needed
They always seemed to get handed to us.
We both throughout the years grew into two unique
Individuals, who always knew exactly what we wanted out of life.
And that was to be friends forever.
One would have thought we were sisters the way we enjoyed
Each other's company,
But eventually it all had to come to an end, that day we
Grew wise and older.
When our true love came into our lives to me was our
Friendship got put on hold,
But a friendship such as ours shall never fade for it will
Be in our hearts for our life time.

Sweetie

His smile is from the suns golden rays
His touch is as gentle as a feather
His voice carries the comfort of the birds chirping
He smells of sweet roses that is dancing through the four winds
To see my Sweetie play carefree is enough for
Me to be a proud grandmother
Terrell is my cane that carries me through my
Darkest days

Dedicated to my first grandson Terrell Blaine

A Daughters Wish

The last days with you are the days I will remember
forever though these days were the toughest for you
Always in so much pain that you could not
tell, but through your eyes did I see it
I prayed with all my heart that God would
heal that pain and make you well
Enough to come home to your family
I guess God had other plans for you, for he did not heal your pain
He made it plain as day that he was taking you away
This I was so hurt for but a moment
When you took your last breath, but my heart realized mother
You will suffer no more and your company shall
be joined with those gone before you
Mother dear I wish you'd be here with me every day
I miss your caring voice that which you
expressed daily to your children
This shall be a memory cherished deep within my heart and mind
Knowing that your spirit is watching over me always
When the light summers showers of rain fall gently down upon us
I know will know that it is you mother dear sprinkling your love
Down over your family who will miss you forever

Ron

Just as plain as day can I see your smiling face, hear your
Forever thoughtful voice,
If it were my choice Ron you'd still be here with the ones who
Love you dear.
With a bit of fear in my mind I can only imagine that I'll
Never see your smiling face or hear your
Caring voice speak to me.
But Ron our love for you shall forever keep our memories of you
Living deep within our hearts, where we'll never be apart.
Those moments we shared with you laughing and confiding
In one another shall we cherish forever,
And those little problems we spoke of we
both knew they were nothing.
Ron life may seem empty without you by our sides, but we all know
Your spirit shall be the guiding light that will carry
Us through our trying times of grief.
Our only relief from this grief
Is too remember the good times we shared with you
Till we meet again Ron, miss you dodo

Cry Not I Ask

As the final pebbles of sand fall through the body of time
I only ask this of you have you a moment of
memory which you remember
My voice ever hurting of all that
I have not accomplished to this day, no
For all that I have done in my life time shall you cherish for every
Tomorrow, and never have that sorrow of
Weeping from my absence,
Feel not the pain of hurt nor anger for there has only been
A ray of light that gracefully carried me through
Those darkened days of always wanting
More out of life, but it seems life has taken more out of
Me, Cry not I ask

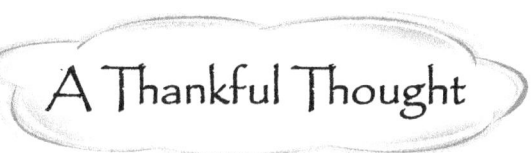

A Thankful Thought

I'm thankful for those who hold a special place in my heart
I'm thankful for the lord up above, for allowing
us to have the things we have
I'm thankful for every breathe I breath
which shows me the importance
Of life
I'm thankful for what life has to offer us as we approach each day
In confidence
I'm thankful for every tomorrow that I greet with
Pride and joy

Deception

Your innocence is a betrayal to your image,
in my eyes you neglect to
Expose the truth, but continue to wonder freely
As I sit and wait your company only
To encounter your deception.
Why can't you be wise when you look into my eyes and see?
What you are doing to me,
I will understand if you'd only confide in me, darling why don't
You tare down those walls that is keeping
Us distant.
Let my love over rule your deceptive behaviour, for my love
Is a burning flame, waiting
To hold you in my arms for but a moment,
Please try just a little harder to open up for this flame will
Slowly burn down waiting for you

Waterfalls

As the cool waters flow down the mountain edge, slashing against
Layers of rock making the breathless
Image of the waterfalls.
While the summers sun gets hotter, harder the waters fall
Creating a cool stream alongside the road
Sparkling like diamonds in the sun, as they gently shimmer
Over the mountain edge, this beauty from
Mother Nature is one for all to enjoy as
Everyone captures it in their eyes
Waterfalls

Space

Drifting through thee uncounted stars, which seems to be in a land
Far from reality,
My mind in so much peace as I sweep through
The moonlit night
This is the space I have been dreaming of to have my mind
At total rest as the best is yet to come.
Oh what a feeling this is, just you and all space filled with
Peace where no human can interface,
I drift for miles in the starry skies with no particular place to go,
Enjoying the freedom.
Why can't I find this space in reality? But only deep in my
Heart and mind where I wonder off
Too.

Summers Walk

As I take my summers walk enjoying all of
nature's creations, which nothing
Can compare to its beauty.
The smell of the wild flowers as they bloom under the
Summers sun is a fragrance only nature can produce.
The gentleness of the winds caressing my skin as I walk and listen
To the birds chirping their beautiful music
Is a feeling of relaxation.
Watching the children playing freely in the play grounds,
Is a wonderful sight as they have no fear in the world.
As I approach the end of my walk I see the summer's sun
Starting to set showing the beautiful colors
Of as sunset that can be seen far over
The horizon.
The peace here is so great one would never think of
Leaving this place, as the sun hits the highest mountain peak
Setting its final glow, I stop for a
Moment to gaze upon its beauty and this brings
My walk to an end.

Common Grounds

Racism such a hard subject to deal with, yet its importance is far to
Valuable to pass, the hurt and
Frustration portrayed by some has caught everyone's attention,
Why? Please tell me why those did
People have to suffer this was brought on by people
Who refused to understand right from wrong,
From the beginning we were all created as equals and were
Thought to be respected and the right to
Live one's life free from discrimination.
From the courage and wisdom of those who got mocked
Because of their nationality, have proved to
The rest of the world that they are the
Blessed ones who never gave up on their faith,
Even though times were tough they stood their ground.
While deep down in their hearts they only wised for the same
Things we so freely enjoy, that
Is freedom to do as they please, we are all equals of
This common ground let the past be forgotten
And go forth in prosper in a
Brand new world.

Silent River

Silently the river flows, softly down the green valley,
Meanwhile a canoe quietly drifts by the river's edge baring with it
One man and his wife, searching
For that virgin land where no man has stepped foot on
For his family to be,
Floating down where the river carries him is where he'll
Plant his seeds to bring forth a new generation of his own,
Shall be known as the sole owner of
His new found land.
As the years pass him by he has aged more than he could
Handle, the time has come for
Him to leave the silent river that brought him a home,
Not long after he left the river runs silent
No more for his people are now
Fighting for their land that is getting
Destroyed by floods.

Raven & Wolf Artwork
by Anthony R. Gosnell

Unity

This world needs all the care we have to offer it, just as we
Care for our loved ones so must we care
for our planet, it is up to human
Society to preserve and nurture it for
Our future generations to come.
Through the understanding of unity that we possess we
Will survive all this destruction that is going on today.
We must teach and share the knowledge to those in doubt.
From that quote: "United we stand "Divided we fall"
This we must never forget.
Let us put a stop to judging others by their nationality, or how
They live their lives, we must
Realize that we share in every form of life as equals.
And take into serious consideration
That those who you mock have feelings just as
You and I.
We must present unity as the threshold of our lives,
And respect those around us no matter
The color of their skin or how they live their lives.
Unity is the way of life for it brings freedom
And love to everyone around the world.

Distant Friends

Distant friend you came from a place far
from m y home, just as I to yours
You were so kind and understanding
As we were both there for a purpose in a land strange to both
Of us, but we certainly made the time
While it lasted.
We experienced the most rewarding and educational convention,
Which we all something in common, the love
Of poetry where we shared, listened and talked
For hours.
A friendship was created far from what I ever expected to find,
Though it was for a few days
Our friendship shall last forever, when the time came for
Us to say our goodbyes, we knowingly knew that
One day our paths will cross.
So farewell my distant friend until that day comes,
Where we will once
Again share our love for poetry.

A Vision

As I was walking down the road, the rain was pouring down to
The ground, I saw a vision, a vision brought to
Me from the past, I saw
Before me the future of our land
In this vision of mine everything was fine as can be, our
People had this glorifying glow that
Could be seen for miles around, there was
A sign of happiness in the air.
For there was no more fighting nor was there any more
Hours of unsettled disputes
This vision brought to us the unity of the land, which
Was held hostage for so many years.
The sun was surely shining down upon this great
Land of ours, as the birds cheerfully sang a song of praise
To welcome this gift of freedom.
The vision of a great victory came upon me,
Asking me to let our people know that the end of our fighting
Is finally at hand, say unto them 'Fear not Nisga'a's:
For the time has come to let the
Fighting spirits of our forefathers lay down to rest
We have won the final stage to victory,
The Land Claims

Bro'

He is young and full of energy that any nine year old can ever have,
There are days when he is so sweet and adorable,
Those days I cherish.
But like any growing boy he is filled with all the curiosity one
Child could explore, asking many questions of
Things he doesn't understand, and having the most outrageous
Remarks one can give.
Through the years of childhood, I will be
there for my Bro, I will teach
Him whatever he needs to know and take him wherever I go.
Every minute that we share together will remain
In my heart for eternity.
From his first cry when as he was brought into this world
To that last laugh he will have
As he remarks on any comment I make to him.
My Bro will always have a very special place in my heart,
I will hold him in my arms and comfort him.
I will make the pain go away and my love will be his security
Blanket, until the day comes and he will
Be on his own, who will become a young man that I wish
To see him as.

My Baby

When my baby talks I listen, when he giggles I laugh too,
For he is my baby
When he is hurt I will kiss his lil ow'we better, just to see
His face light up with his tender smile
For his pain is my pain also.
When he wants to learn I will teach him all that he needs to know
So when that day arrives and he is on his own
He'll need only the knowledge I taught him.
When he wants a new toy to play with, I will buy him whatever
His heart desires, for he is my pride and joy.
I know that he will only be my baby for a few short years,
And those years I will cherish deep in my heart
That when he is older and wiser, he will
Realize that his mommy loved him ever so dear
My baby......Shane

I Remember

I remember your smile that would light up our skies
Hear your voice when
You called on those rainy days, you'd always say
Hi Sis' what sup, oh how I remember
Those days.
I remember how much you offered even though there wasn't much.
I remember the gentleness
You showed to your children and in their eye's did we
See how much they loved you.
I love to remember all the good times we shared, I'll always
Remember you Brother Ron

Raining on our Love Artwork
by Merlin C. Robinson

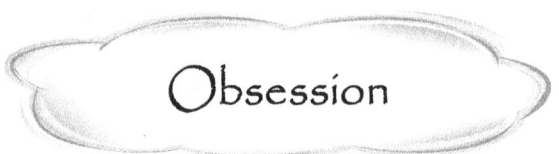

Obsession

To love is to be obsessed with the one who means the world to you
You share everything there is to share with them.
Your love has that unbreakable bond that
Keeps you united.
While deep within your heart you pray nothing or no one
Will come between you, for you are
Totally obsessed with your perfect love.
The uniqueness of the love you share there is no other
Like it.
For your obsession proved that love will conquer all your fears
And doubts.
As our hearts collide exploding with a passionate fore
Of love,
As we are destined to be together for eternity for this obsession
Is the foundation of a wonderful relationship,
To love is to care, to care is to share
To share is to be obsessed with a perfect love.

Truth

The truth is a hard thing to confront, but its importance is the
Threshold of a relationship,
The more you neglect to tell the truth further your
Relationship will dissolve.
If you think you are protecting yourself, by holding back
What needs to be told, you are only
Fooling yourself that will bring more pain.
As time goes by you will realize that any relationship
Is based on pure honesty and commitment,
Without these you bring insecurity between you.
Never dwell on the truth what needs to be told tell it,
Whether it be good or bad once spoken
Your mind will be at ease.
Always be open with one another, bring down
Those walls that create problems.

Pain and Happiness

Pain is watching the world dissolve in war
And hunger,
While happiness is watching our children grow
Up without a fear in mind.
Pain is watching people abuse drugs and alcohol
Which will eventually destroy them.
Happiness is someone being there to help them
Overcome their passion for
The drugs.
Pain is watching a loved one being taken away from
Family and friends, because of no cure
For their illness.
Happiness is having to spent as much time with them
Caring and sharing for them as they
Quietly slip away.
Pain is watching family lose all hope and faith, because
They don't have the money to care
For their children.
Happiness is by a stroke of luck that family gets blessed
With all that they need.
Happiness is watching the pain go away.

Two Ships

We are like two ships passing in the night, as the
Four winds gently guide us
Over the open sea, with no particular place to go,
Just sailing in the moonlit night.
With the reflection of the silver moon lighting up
Our paths brings us much closer
To each other.
The night is still and quiet not a sound to be heard
Only the gentle howling of the four winds,
The stars are like diamonds that light up the heavens
Up above us, twinkling ever so bright.
As we sail past the moon gazing up into the sky
A falling star catches our eyes watching
It slowly glide across the sky.
As the moon sets its final glow and slowly descends
Into the ocean floor, bringing to end
The most perfect night one can ask for, there
We must part our sails for
Our paths has come to an end.

Pressures

Every days mere trials build up, may they be good
Or bad, each bind a wall of content inside of me a wall
So high and strong that
There are times I refuse to see past it.
If only I had someone to talk to, someone who
Will listen, someone who will always
Be there for me, especially give me the advice
I seek.
My problems may seem small to some people,
But I am forced to live each day in
Life's pressures that are fighting inside
Of me.
I must tare down these walls that are building
Up inside of me, friend or no friend
I must not let this destroy my life,
I must release all of the pressures that have
I depressed.

Be Cool

One of life's accomplishment is to stay away
From three tempting habits,
That is made available anywhere
And to everyone
That is Alcohol, drugs unprotected sex.
Once you have been exposed to them there
Is no guarantee that you'll say no the next time.
If you are trapped into it because
Your friends are doing it,
Think twice for when you hit the bottom
Your friends are gone, and there is
No one there to pick you up,
So be cool and stay away from this kind of life,
Don't be a fool and play with your
Future, life is too important to waste on little
Pleasures that last for a few minutes
Or hours, you'll be faced with
Regrets

Dreams

You are always in my dreams, I can see your
Lonely face waiting for me
To walk down that long dark road of
Dreams.
Grandfather is there something you are trying
To tell me? Or are you warning me,
Of some kind of danger.
Every time I try to talk to you, I am awakened
By the fear of knowing that
You are no longer with us in body,
Dreams can be a communication break through,
If you have the ability to read a dream,
To understand their meaning
You are a gifted person.
Grandfather is it you are telling me to let go,
To accept the fact that you are gone
But will live forever in
Our memories.

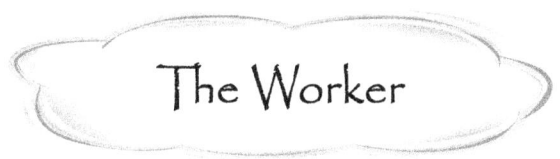

The Worker

He awakes before the birds start singing their cheerful
Songs, makes his lunch and coffee
To last him through the day.
When he is done he washes himself, puts on his
Work clothes, as he quietly
Comes into the room to kiss me good bye,
Then he is gone for the day, working
So hard with only the company
Of his machine.
He is such a hard worker, works through the
Hot summers sun, cold winter days,
On a job he enjoys so much,
As his work day comes to an end, he makes
His way home to the love of his life,
The worker.

Our Love

In the beginning there was just the two of us,
So much in love, tried so much to
Never be apart.
The years passed by as we planted our seeds,
That produced our family,
We loved and cared for each of them, with all
The love we had to offer.
Our love was a fire burning inside us, keeping
Our relationship alive.
As each day approached us, we greeted it
With a smile as it brought us much closer
To each other.
If there was ever a rainy day where we felt
There was no hope, the sun was
Sure to shine down upon us, for we were
Meant to be together,
Through the good times as well as the bad,
Our love is the foundation
That is holding this love together, only
A love as strong as ours
Will conquer whatever we encounter,
Our Love.

Godmother

She is a special person to me, her vow to take care
Of me, brought a bond between us,
That I will respect her always.
If there are days that you do not realize that I'm
Very thankful to have you as a part of my life,
Though we rarely speak,
My prayers are with you as in some sense
You are like a mother to me,
So shall my children grow to know you
Godmother may the lord send down blessed rays
Of sunshine to light up your days.
The times you gave me advice that brought
My life back on track, when I was
At a point in my life I didn't want to care, you
Were there to show me that it's my
Life and I must cherish it
As I cherish life my children.
Godmother I really appreciate your understanding and
Love you express to me.

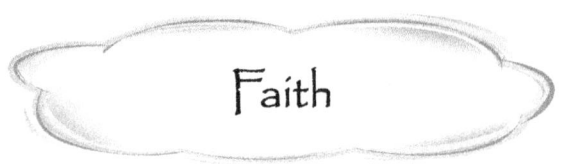

Faith

Living of my faith is what I do daily, I have no valuable
Possessions to be proud of,
Only the clothes on my back that are not made of
Fine fabric,
I try not to weep for the things I long for, why shed
Tears for the things you can only
Hope for.
When you hold in the palm of your hands, the most
Important thing in life that is Love.
Love the one thing money can't buy, living of
My faith and having all the love I need
Is the only happiness I can ask for?
Let your faith keep you alive.

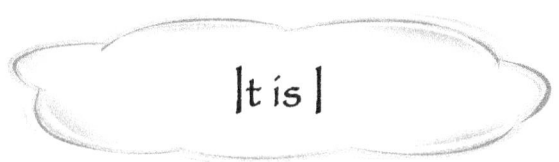

It is

The finest things around can be the cruelest ones, you
Shall walk through each day of you
Life hoping that nothing will ever go wrong,
But to your surprise everyone you
Trusted have turned the tables to bring
You down.
But don't frown or feel that there is no one
Around, for it is I your truest friend,
I was there when your heart was aching, I was
There watching you faking your happiness,
I was there when the sun turned
Into darkened skies, when
You had no one to hold and comfort you
As you trembled in the cold night.
It is I that carried you through each of your
Trying times, I am your inner being
Your most trusted friend.
I am you and you are me.

Nkwana

Our lives are so distant, yet our voices can be heard
Plain as the stars shine, on the moons
Flight at night.
A million miles separate out chances of hugging one
Another, but do we let that stop
Our love of communicating?
No, I can hear the gentleness of your voice and
The love you have for your family,
As you write your letters to fill me in on your
Life far across the other side of the world.
Was through faith that our lives became connected,
Was it chance that you are
Now my daughter, whatever it be that brought
Our hearts together,
I thank my lucky stars showing me the path to follow,
That linked our two countries together
Through the link of our pens, we are uniting our
Love as well as our two worlds,
That are so far apart.
Nkwana your smile lights up my sky
A million miles away.

Dedicated to my adopted daughter in
Africa.

Beauty of the Night

Driving over the muddy pot hole roads of the lava beds,
The night was quiet and calm,
While up above the muddy roads were stars that
Hung gently in the sky.
Not far on the left, Hale Bopp caught my eye
Clear and bright as a picturesque image.
As we marvelled upon its closeness to earth,
We were also blessed to gaze upon the moon that
Had a strange look tonight.
We starred timelessly at such beauty, which followed
Us as we drove, but each time we looked
Again the beauty was by far
More beautiful, the reddish orange flared out rays
Into the blue sky, the greyish power started
Overlapping the bright half of the moon,
To our surprise we realized we are witnessing
An eclipse, behold the beauty of the
Universe was bestowed upon us tonight.
On our left gently hanging in the heavens and on the
Right transforming before our eyes,
Was the eclipse, what more can we be offered,
But the beauty of the night to
Delight our eyes.

Love Me

Love me like I've never been loved before, walk with
Me through those doors of infinity,
Where there is nothing more but the purity
Of inner emotions.
Hold me in thy arms, oh sweet one of mine
Caress me till the night falls quietly
Over the hot summers sun.
What else can I say? But to love me with all thine
Heart, so we'll never be apart,
Oh love of mine.
Speak unto me the true meaning of love, and just
How much I mean to you, give me the
Security and passion I need.
Let us stroll through the garden of memories, where
We once laid down our heads together,
Amongst the sweet smell of the wild flowers.
Where our passion flowed through each
Unique peddle that gently hung together, as our love
So gracefully enhanced the beauty
Of each flower.
Love me, walk with me and talk with me so the
World can see how much we mean to
One another, my love may these moments
Last for eternity.

Joy of My Life

The sweet nectar of a golden delicious fills the air
With each bite;
So are you the joy of my life!
As the colors of spring blossoms freely, each
Day bring forth the birth of a new beginning;
So are you the joy of my life!
The feeling of the warm sun that
Gently falls down upon my body;
So are you the joy of my life!
As the birds chirp quietly outside my window,
Early in the morning's dew;
So are you the joy of my life
The fruit that bears the beauty of time
Is the innocent voice of tomorrow?
So are you the joy of my life.

Dedicated to my 3 children and grandchildren.

A Christmas Wish

Everything was planned, everything seemed so surreal.
The family dinner planned, the gifts all bought,
But did I see the silent fights,
The slightest hints, No

Until Christmas Eve, here comes nothing, here comes
Silence, of words not spoken,
But actions taken,

My heart is breaking, my spirit broken with no words spoken.
My family, can you hear me, can you feel
The pain, oh how much it aches,

As I see how much hate you have, how much you have
Forgotten, the true meaning of our family gatherings,
My wish now, I wish for our Christmas to be
The way our Mother made it feel, when she was here.

I wish for peace and I wish for happiness for my
Family on this Christmas Eve

A Love Found But Lost

We met online for the first time,
Which seemed to be mutual feelings sent thru Cyber space.

As I looked at your face, I seen in you eye's for
A moment, I seen that shy person you spoke
Quietly of, dancing freely trying to break thru.

You asked; what did I see in you? Bestowed my lonely
Heart when we first met, you gave me the security
To trust another in this heart of mine.

The moments we shared together, are moments that can
Never be forgotten, as I laid in your arms,
I heard our heart beat speak of passion,
Our bodies caressed as our lips locked
In a kiss far beyond the Starz can explain.

Then came what I feared the most, are the words that
Brought on a heartache that shed a million
Tears, for the Love I found is the love I lost.......
All I wish for is to have those moments back
To make it last

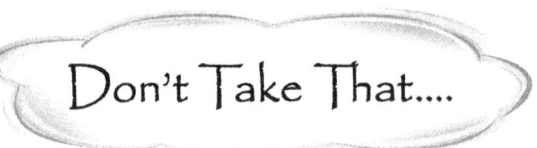

Don't Take That....

Cuts will heal, bruises will fade away
What can I say, words spoken that are meant to hurt a person?
Are words of cowardliness, I will not stand by and watch;
As a loved one is continually degraded,
Love is what you make it, love is what you give,
I know you give it your all "Don't take that"
To watch and not say anything is by far
the worst thing a friend can do,
We must take a stand and stop this abusive pattern,
We must call that friend and say
'Don't take that"…

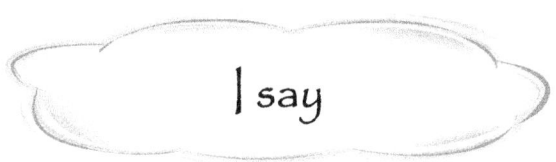

If I never said, how much I Love You, What I see in you, what I feel!!

There is a time and a place I go to in my mind, to be close to you

Babe,

I can see the sun rise, I can see the moon set,
in your arms is where I want to be,

When I see the Love in your eyes, it brings a tear to my eye,

To know the Love you feel for me, and the love I give back to you,

Is by far every emotion I feel!

I Say this from my heart because

Babe who are we and where are we going?

What is love? Where is Love?

Where is this going to take us?

I say............

Killerwhale Artwork
by Albert M. Stephens

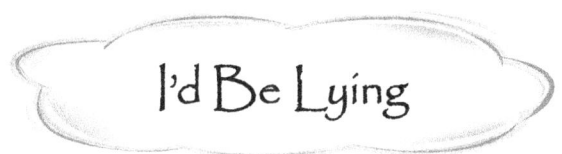

I'd Be Lying

I'd be lying if I said I was Ok, I'd be lying if I said I was happy.

As I lay here at night, thinking of the moments we shared

I'm scared that these memories shall fade as

The Stars fade into the winter's dawn

Everything seemed so right, as my heart was in such a delight,

As each night passed us by, the love grew stronger

To the bond we were creating,

My mind started wandering, as the tears started flowing down

My face, so did I hide my face in the pillow,
where you once laid your head.

What's to be said? For was this all but a lie, as I started to cry harder

So did my heart break even more, but we both knew

Once more that this love could never be
the one we wanted the most,

So let us part as we started, being friends.

Let the memories be just that, something
to cherish, and look back at

That we lived in a lie of deception

Filled with love and passion

If I Could

If I could bring back all those nights and days we shared.

I Would Babe, I remember every lil word you spoke,
Every lil jester you made,

To see that smile, hear your voice would be priceless,
Babe you are one that will forever be in our hearts,
Just as the sunshine's, the moon rises,
And the Starz hang gracefully in the universe

If I could hold you in my realm

Love is Mystical

Love is mystical, love is tranquility,
And Love is a ray of sunshine on a cloudy day,
Love is deeper than the ocean,
Love is Angels dancing amongst the stars;
As your heart beat dances in mine babe.
To feel Love like ours is beyond my realm,
I lost love once but in you I found Love again.
Happy Valentines to my Sweet Heart
Dedicated to Frankie G

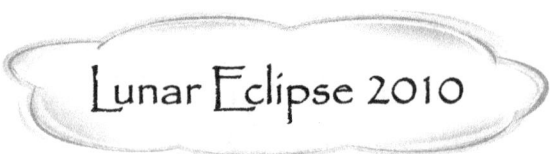

Lunar Eclipse 2010

On a cold winter's night of December I prepared
myself for a night to remember,
The Lunar Eclipse of 2010.

So did the world wait in aw, as we sat in my car
IPod on hand posting as the first stages began,

Binoculars in the other, the transformation was by far the

Most beautiful sight, each picture taken, I posted to share

For those unfortunate not able to witness

The miraculous event of the universe.

Posts from the world around started hitting Facebook, pictures

Of every magnitude portrayed the Lunar Eclipse of 2010

As the second stage hit, the night grew colder, as I stood outside

To take pictures was for a moment as my

Hands froze, my breath drew spears of ice as I breathed in awe.

Then came the final stage as the sun crossed silently

Over the moon, the color changed to a blood red, that so quietly

Brought out all wanders of the mind and universe,

As time elapsed, so did the Lunar Eclipse take total control

Of a December's Winter Night

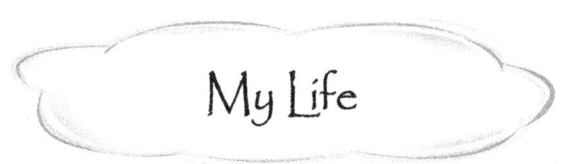

My Life

What can I say, but I want my life back, as I look in my past

Everything was going so fine, all I did was, live it

To the fullest.

Tried never to hurt a soul, helped those who needed help.

Then out of the dreary summer's sky, the darkened

Clouds rolled in, hung in the sky over my head, waiting to

Strike like a thunder bolt which jolted the axles of my world,
That spun me in a turmoil.

From that day forward things in my life
were never the same, and who's

To blame? I ask this question, who's to blame.

I had a job that secured my family, had the family that secured

The foundation of love and life.

Now the job is gone, so is everything I worked so hard to build,

My strength and faith has grown weaker, as I try desperately to put

My Life back together.........all I want is

To be sane and not live in pain.

My Life

My Love for You Both

My love Wish you were here, wish I can hold you
Wish I could say I Love you

If God has a plan I wish for you I want to be there

Where you guys are, miss you so much
And want to be there holding you, talking and laughing

I so remember the days and nights we sat there talking

Laughing, crying, Miss you both.........

My heart has never felt as heavy as it is today
My love miss you forever.

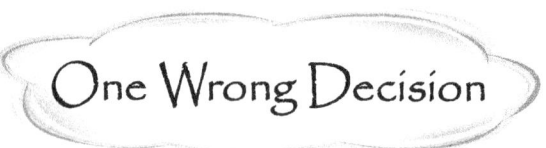

One Wrong Decision

One wrong decision, that caused my life to come to a halt
I thought I had no fault
But to my astonishment, came a case of Action to Reaction
As I heard from their reaction, I did
something I shouldn't have done,
As they continued to talk I was stunned to know
how my Actions affected those I love.
Those who seen potential in me,
lil did I acknowledge my decision, as a wrong one,
To those I hurt, to those who care enough to be by my side,
Please for my Actions,
I promise not to walk this path again, should I fall from it,
I know you'll be right there to pick me up,
Plant my feet on the right path again

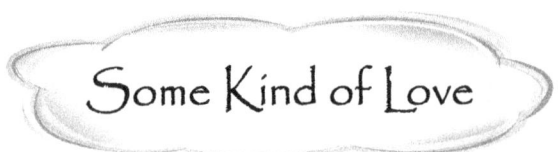

Some Kind of Love

Baby you take my breath away, from the moment I laid eyes on you,
Baby I knew one day we would be together
As you walked by me I seen it in your eye's
that fate will make our paths cross.
It has being two years, oh how our loved has blossomed,
Every minute we are apart, brings us that much closer together
We have
Gone through good and bad, our love carried us over each
Obstacle. Thank you for being my crutch, my love, my life
Baby this is some kind of love, a love I thought I would never find
Again, a love I will cherish far beyond this realm,
This is our destiny to be as one, from this day forward.
My Love will be in your heart, my life shall be an open book for you
As we share, as we create some kind of love.

Tonight

The day started as we wanted it to be, the Night OMS what to

Expect, as we drove over the somewhat cloudy skies,

In my eyes you sat there, watching, waiting
for a reaction in my emotion,

Tonight we'll be together for the first time, as us

Some say we are who we are, never think
twice of exactly who you are

Tonight I'm going to make you feel the way I feel, See what we see

Hear what we want to hear, tonight is going to last forever,

As we fall asleep, you are the one I want in my
arms, you are the one I want to see

When I wake up, they say Love has no
boundaries but babe what we share
Tonight is going to last forever, beyond this Realm

Tonight..................

CPSIA information can be obtained
at www.ICGtesting.com
Printed in the USA
BVHW042101080722
641517BV00002B/10